HEALING RHYMES

Poetry of a Resurrected Man

RECOMMENDED

THE BUDDING WARRIOR

This publication contains the opinions and ideas of its author. It is intended to provide helpful and informative material on the subjects addressed in the publication. The author and publisher specifically disclaim all responsibility for any liability, loss or risk, personal or otherwise, which is incurred as a consequence, directly or indirectly, of the use and application of any of the contents of this book.

WORKBOOK PRESS LLC
187 E Warm Springs Rd,
Suite B285 Las Vegas NV 89119 USA

Website: https://workbookpress.com/
Hotline: 1-888-818-4856
Email: admin@workbookpress.com

Ordering Information:

Quantity sales. Special discounts are available on quantity purchases by corporations, associations, and others. For details, contact the publisher at the address above.

Library of Congress Control Number:

ISBN-13:   978-1-965732-45-8   Paperback Version

REV. DATE: 12/07/2024

HEALING RHYMES

Poetry of a Resurrected Man

The Budding Warrior

ACKNOWLEDGEMENT

My deepest appreciation goes to everyone who encouraged me, prayed for me, and supported this project—whether through words, work, or finances. Without you, this book wouldn't be here.

I dedicate this book to my late father, Charles Robert Bateman, and my mother, Naomi Ruth Bateman, who didn't hesitate to set me straight when I needed it most. I also honor the memory of my dear sister, Debbie Bateman.

To my brothers—Robert, John, and Clark—thank you for being not only family but true friends. To Paul Aspacio, to Robert and his wife Denise, and to my beautiful daughter, Renquel, you each hold a special place in my heart.

To Paul and Margaret Terhaar: you absolutely blew me away with your amazing illustrations. They're bold, brilliant, and straight-up unforgettable. Paul, thank you for your friendship, encouragement, and for helping me land on the perfect title. Margaret, thank you for being such a positive influence and steady presence—you make everything better just by being there. I love and appreciate you both more than words can say.

Many thanks also to Ms. Jessica Johnson, Ms. Janet, June from medical, Jesse, and Ray Ray—your kindness hasn't gone unnoticed.

And most importantly, my endless gratitude to my Lord and Savior, Jesus Christ, for His grace and companionship every step of the way, and to the Holy Spirit, who faithfully guided me through this assignment.

LETTER FROM THE AUTHOR

I am a 61-year-old man who grew up in a deeply religious home. My father served as a minister for 20 years before his passing in 1982, and I am the youngest of three brothers. My sister, whom I loved dearly, passed away in 2009. Though I never finished high school, I later earned my GED, and I have always believed that learning comes in many forms.

For 14 years, I made a modest living as a metal fabricator. Today, I am retired and share my home with my brother Robert and his wife, Denise, who mean the world to me. I also find joy and companionship in my three dogs—Ruger, Coppertone, and Forest.

This is my sixth book, following the path of my earlier works, though this one carries a new title that I truly love. What makes this poetry collection unique is that it not only features my own writing but also includes illustrations, drawings, and images contributed by both myself and friends.

My life has not been without struggles. I battled addiction for many years, and those were some of the darkest chapters of my journey. Yet, in the midst of brokenness, I found light through writing poetry, creating art, and turning my focus toward the good things in life. This book reflects that journey—of healing broken hearts, encouraging the hopeless, and offering compassion to those in need.

The road back to a better path has been challenging, but it has also been transformative. My hope is that these poems will speak to you, inspire you, and perhaps even touch your life in a way that reminds you of the power of grace, healing, and hope.

With gratitude,
Charles Bateman

ABOUT THE AUTHOR

I am 61 years old and grew up in a deeply religious home. My father, who served as a minister, tragically took his own life in 1982. I am the youngest of three surviving brothers, and in 2009, I lost my beloved sister. Though I never graduated from high school, I later earned my GED and worked for many years as a metal fabricator in HVAC air and heating. Today, I am retired and live with my brother Robert and his wife, Denise, whom I love dearly. I also share my life with three loyal companions—my dogs Ruger, Coppertone, and Forest—who are truly my best friends.

Writing has been my passion and lifeline. Over the years, I've published five books of poetry: Twisted Spiritual Poetry (volumes 1 & 2) and Memoirs and Poems of a Misguided Junkie. This is my fourth book, and while it stands on its own, it carries the heart and spirit of my earlier works. What makes this collection unique is the inclusion of both my own illustrations and those of friends—art woven together with words to create something deeply personal.

I have faced many battles, including years of addiction, which were among the darkest times of my life. Yet out of that pain came poetry—an outlet for healing, a voice of encouragement for the hopeless, and a way to give back to those in need. This book is a reflection of that journey: from brokenness toward redemption, from despair toward hope.

Life is not always easy. The path we walk can be hard, lonely, and exhausting. But we are never truly alone—we have a God, a Savior, and the Holy Spirit watching over us, guiding us, and urging us forward. My prayer is that these poems bless you with healing, hope, and even moments of humor along the way.

Gratefully,
Charles Bateman

Life is good and I'm happy to be alive. God bless you all need to understand your value, you are gifted, blessed, you are worthy to be loved, and respected. The path we're traveling can be hard, lonely, tiresome,. Well, you get what I'm saying, but we have A God, A savior, The Holy Spirit, whom watches over us, protects us, gently pushing us toward the edge where we can jump up and fly or basically fall to our death, so let's be careful out there.

May these poems bless you with healing, hope and humor.

- The Budding Warrior

THIS BOOK IS ALSO DEDICATED TO THE MEMORY OF MY GREAT DAD

Charles Robert Bateman

He is my father, a minister, loving husband, and a responsible dad.

AUTHOR'S ACTUAL PICTURES DURING THE TUCSON BOOK FAIR 2024 BOOK SIGNING EVENT

My poetry brought me from Washington State to Tucson Arizona. There, I did a book signing convention. My second book "Memoirs and poems of a misguided junkie" were signed and given away just to get my profile established. It was loads of fun and just so nice down there. I'm not the greatest poet by any means but I do my best and hopefully I'll get better in time.

♥ The Budding Warrior ♥

WE JUST NEVER KNOW

I was standing on the corner, minding my business,
My shoes were tattered, and frail

Across the street, there were hooker's presiding,
Blowjob's and pussy for sale

As I made my way to a house, torn and abandoned,
something was drawing me in

I'd thought to myself, my luck here is changing,
finally I was set up to win

I came to a room with a cot and a mattress,
what a blessing, a fine place to sleep

As I drifted off,, right there on the bed dreaming,
I could feel a hand under the sheet

As I opened my eyes, I was stiff as a board,
The hair on my neck stood up straight

In a deep, frightening voice, it said " I am your calling "
I feed on your fear's, and your hate

He went on to say, that he was a spirit, paving
his way to my soul,

His whisper was wrenched, you'd not want to hear it
I was helpless, he gained all control

He pulled off my sheet, he began to possess me,
I pleaded, God come set me free!

But it was too late, he had all of the power,
He had the lock and the key

He controlled my body, my facial expressions
for now I was under his spell

He used me to rape, rob kill, and plunder,
and for me, the next stop is hell.

THE SECT YOU LIKE TO EAT

There in the east is a mountain,
home to a dark kind of sect

Their shelters carved in stone were
impressive, they're statues were broken
and wrecked

As our party invested in finding the tribe there,
something just didn't
make sense

Night came upon us quite sudden,
we made a fire and put up our tent's

As morning came we heard someone crying,
We got up to see who was there

What we discovered was gripping
and frightening
body parts strewn everywhere

The tribe called "the Ute" mutilated,
their ears, eye's, and tongue's in a
pot

Just then a skater named Larry,
yelled, mealtime, let's eat while it's hot!

Thought you could all
take part in a giggle.

ROAD TRIP

Highway 21 was eternal, cut through
the rocks and the hills

A sign meant to be a stern warning,
of a hitcher that kidnaps and kill's

I came to a diner in this desert,
it seemed like an old dumb cliche

A waitress called Kate was a talker,
and she had a whole lot to say

She spoke on a small darling family,
I could see fear in her eye's

She said as she was closing the diner,
she heard their blood chilling cries

The sheriff pulled in to the crime scene,
what he saw brought a chill up his spine

They were pinned to the wall with a nail gun,
Their lips were sewn shut with some twine

There on the fridge was a message,
saying' I will be killing again

If was the question they were asking,
the question should have been when

If you get the itch for a road trip,
don't travel down highway 21

You may end up with a sewn lip
pinned to the wall with
an old, rusty nail gun.

Poetry

JUST FOR NOW

All alone in a world full of chaos, where the
shadows are standing in line.

There a break in the clouds, such a wonder,
the strangers are pretty, and kind.

When I grow tired of the pain I am holding,
when the line that is frail starts to break.

I look deep down within secret places,
there I find all the shit I can't take.

One day I will know hidden mysteries,
I'll solve riddles that capture the heart,

Time will not dwell there in heaven,
And our loved ones no longer apart.

BAD COMPANY

Rolling down the track on the black train,
with no shoe's upon my feet.
People will tell you I'm insane, the kind you
don't want to meet.
Take me back to the river, drown me in
the rift while we're there.
As my body shakes with a quiver, sell me
but buyer beware.
The darkness is where you can find me, in
a realm where the succubus sleep, there the
devil reminds me, that I belong in the " keep "
I was predisposed to a bad seed, I'm a killer
when the low tide turns red.
I function in the night, do a bad deed, some
think I'd be better off dead
The moral to this story is simple, be careful of the
stranger you meet,
When I approach there, you may feel a ripple,
you're the kind of food I like
to eat.

CHAT WITH A DEMON

" Mary, and her meeting she
had with a demon "
Mary was a small town girl, she had a boyfriend,
they hung out at the grange every Saturday night
and danced to the slap your knee music.
Until' one night she and her friends were having a sleep
over, they were daring her to go to the old
Thompson house, said to have a sinister energy
looming from the cracks in the walls.
The very next night Mary decided to see for herself,
As she came to the front door, she heard a whisper,
it said' " RUN " but she felt compelled to stay, this is what
happened next.

Mary; Hello? anyone there?

Harbinger; Hello Mary, please sit, let's have
a little chat.

Mary; About what exactly?

Harbinger; Let's talk about your fear, it drips off
of your soul like sweat on the brow.

Mary; Yes" I am very much afraid of you
and where you may be from.

Harbinger; I am from the beginning of time, I was
an angel under the most high.
My name was Harbinger, I use to sing praises to
the great I AM.

Mary; What are you called now?

Harbinger; My name became Legion, I possess the
strength of a thousand lightning bolts,
I'm also known " in realms unseen as " destroyer.

Mary; How did you become thee demon in charge
of a legion?

Harbinger; There was a war in heaven, a third of us angels
decided to follow Lucifer, the most beautiful
angel there was. We lost the war there and God changed
our beautiful form into grotesque, and vile mutations.

Harbinger; Pray tell Mary, are you frightened?
I know you're scared, but are you gripped with terror?
Answer true, I will know if you lie.

Mary; Harbinger, I am not afraid anymore, though you
are frightening, My faith is in the most high,
He is my protection, my shield.

Harbinger; Yes Mary, you have been anointed, You
bare God's mark on your forehead, He watches
every step you take.

Mary; I pray, the next face I see, will belong to
Jesus, My Rock.

Harbinger; Your faith is admirable, I have
enjoyed our little chat, all things come
to pass, as our time here.

Mary; Goodbye Harbinger, I wish I could
have seen you before the transformation,
I'll bet you were glorious.

Harbinger; Goodbye Mary, I'll be watching
you.

CHOICE

The populous is growing weary, the times
we find ourselves in are at best unsure and
questionable.
The technology we have developed is impressive,
but' I'm ever reminded that it might be this worlds
downfall.
It is my one wish, that we, meaning every human being
on this planet, learn to live and let live.
LOVE is an eternal word meant to uplift
every person on this rock we call earth.
There is enough room for everyone.
Choice is a privilege

THE DREAMS I'VE SEEN LATELY

The dreams I've seen lately,
the vision's partake,

My fame and fortune,
at the bottom of a lake.

" Empty " your promise,
the vow you forsook,

The friendship you damaged,
the end of our book.

Now is the season, now is all I have,
no thought's for tomorrow,

For now I am glad.

YOU DECIDE

Riding the shoulder, the crest of the end,
shatter my window, in hell we descend.

Rising in daybreak, mapping the way,
lost at the entrance, mouth full of decay.

High in the tower, locked away in a cell,
with lips sewn together, no stories to tell.

The life we imagined, the plans we have made,
death very sudden, in the ground we hath laid.

All of our fortune, our servants, our slaves,
our way of life over, the end of our days.

This letter I've written, it's fragrance is gone,
it's meaning escapes me, as I linger on.

TRUTH

My fire has taken leave, my curiosity has dwindled
down to an unsatisfying " hmm "

Faith, when mixed with the pleasures of this world,
has a way of shrinking, tuning out the still, gentle
voice of our creator.

How I miss the warmth of the Holy Spirit, comforting,
reassuring and steadfast.

Now, The valley of decision is wrought with
those teetering, ashamed of what others might think
if they heard the realness in my voice.

It may serve to get back to the basics of life,
to stand without shame, proud, but clothed in
humility,

the divine Lord I choose to call
"Jesus " the son of the one, the only living
God.

Take this as a cry to return to my heavenly father,
to renew the faith that has no boundaries,
May my aim be on him,

The only Lord that had the edacity to sacrifice his
life for the entirety, the evil, the wicked, the liars,
the tax collectors, the heavy weight of our sin's
upon his shoulders.

The precious LAMB OF GOD.
Jesus Christ.

SHAKING TIME

The edge of the darkness, the crack on the lid,
The owl at the window, my fears as a kid.

When father was shouting, as my mother cried,
as I witnessed him slap her, my love for him died.

The chains that still bind me, the hate I possess,
infringing on reason, one big nasty mess.

The stakes are much higher, the takers I loathe,
constantly begging, a weight I can't tow.

Let this be my lesson, my one shaking cry,
to silence those talking, and leaving them dry.

ANY ONES GUESS

All things that come, shortly will pass
I'll take the good and the bad

We will have trials, the troubles in twos
problems to drive us all mad

Greetings we speak, polite and forthcoming,
spewing the garbage like rain

Buyer beware, the natives are drumming,
I've not the time to explain

This is my feeling, raw and dismissive,
what more is there really to say

As for this wall, high, never ending,
will fall on the road down the way.

IN THE MIRROR I GAZE

Death my companion, death be my guide,
rest now in the shadow's, slaughter my pride.

Death my retainer, my due's must be paid,
death now is calling, for this bed I have made.

As I gaze at the mirror, death now I see,
death wise all knowing, is waiting for me.

Life had its beauty, but my life has past,
Life had its wonder's, but life never last's.

Thou art immortal, in realms sight unseen,
Death cut me a bargain, At the age of
fourteen.

MY FEELING ON THE MATTER

I feel the foundation, strong, undiminished, eternal.
Those lines, along the side, adds to its character,
not bending, not weak as some might think.

The undeniable reason I'm speaking on this, is to
let those who clammer, those who taunt and harass,
and those who mock her, will find themselves crushed
under her fantastically, over powering weight.

The broom of reform is broken.
The ideas of the past should be left there,
we as a nation are at each other's throats.

People, Now is the time we are living,
The most underrated word in our vocabulary,
the one life changing proclamation,
with the power to bring unequivocally,
unbranded change, is LOVE.

AN ALIENS PERSPECTIVE

I am an anomaly, my structure is bound
by a systematic goodness of fit.
If you haven't guessed yet, I am not
of this world, my home is millions of light years
toward the gamma quadrant.
You are not able to understand my language,
You would need a bio capacitor to see me in my
alien form.
I have no skeletal structure, because of that, morphing
from my alien form to that of a
human is difficult but doable.
My presence has been on your
planet for three hundred thousand years,
I witnessed Jesus being crucified, I witnessed
Hitler, and the systematic annihilation of the Jew's.
I was present when the antichrist came to dominate
the world.
As things are, I am not able to reveal myself,
it is not allowed.
I have come to believe that Jesus is your only
salvation.
The choice is yours.

respectfully,
Zod

MY PROCLAMATION

Taring the very fabric, playing with synthetism,
arranging the walls around the populous
to look as if they were our friend

But the feeling they give off, the total sum
of their purpose, causes one to speculate,
pulling, and pushing, continuously these wall's,

breaking, falling over each other, the net value
of their existence, " stop a minute " where
am I going with this? how about accountability,
someone taking responsibility for all the havoc!

Very soon the impenetrable, the invisible Allie
we call the status quo, reassuring the populous,
causing us to sleep without being afraid of
the boogey man.

Now is the time for action, people coming
together with one motive " our safety "

I don't know about you, but I'm tired, sick
in the gut from worry, from doubt, from the
illusion that everything will work itself out!

But hey" what do I know,
I'm just here for the show.

THE CHIP AND THE SPINE

With their hatred pushed to the ends of my nerve's,
I learned to harness it and to use it against them.
I found my calling when they surgically removed my fear,
raising up in me a warrior's courage.
I vowed to cut the rotten heart's out of their hollow chest's.
With every atom spliced to a chip, cut into my spine between
the facet joints.
the chip could control my limbs, my fighting abilities, all
of my motor skills.
Syncing was now possible, every molecule, all of the laminin,
working to create the perfect assassin,
Who could have guessed that all of this was a viable solution?

The neurospecialist is anonymous

The next page yet to be transmitted.

Dark days, no end in sight

In this you will not brim with pleasure,
tilt of lid, deprived of grace

Here you may see other's suffering,
I thought you'd come have a taste

Imagine time's when we moved slower,
satisfied, a job well done

Now the noose is hanging higher
the clock strikes twelve, a child's hung

Forget the damsel in the tower,
the plague has come to rot her flesh

For this you see is the witching hour,
The righteous and the wicked mesh

As of now, your lost and seething,
choking on the bone you ate

Please stop crying, we know your bleeding,
your six behind, you'll have to wait.

RABBIT HOLE

I ride the waves of a current unseen,
tumbling down on an acid machine

I can see my good fortune, a button and pill,
I witnessed my pleasure up high on a hill

The rabbit hole lingered, while I took a dose,
A monkey was running, did not see the post

I spotted two demons up high in a tree,
weaving two pentagrams
out of branches for me

You'd think it was over, it didn't end there,
demons are nasty, they never play fair

What then came next? three loud pound's on the door,
those fucker's were tricky, came up through the floor

What I discovered, served me some toast,
keep the company of demons, you'll have
to play host.

IF MY HEART WAS AN ENGINE

In my engine, a build-up of carbon,
the carburetor hissing with smoke

Blow it all out, be patient, don't shout!
now your engine will run with no choke.

As for its appearance, the car wash is waiting,
now spray off the dust and the mud.

Use car wax and buff, use all of that stuff,
be rid of the dirt and the crud.

NINE MONTHS OF HELL

I haven't the knowledge that you will require,
the time I was baptized, I walked through the fire

Every pore on my body was aching and burning,
as I slowly suffered, the world kept on turning

As for the moment, I only remember,
it was iced cold in June, it felt like December

This was a time for weeping and crying,
my face distorted was shifting and prying

Dying for comfort, I cut a bargain, I'd trade my
soul for a break, for a pardon

For nine months of hell, I was freed from my misery,
a pain not forgotten, hell then released me.

THE VOICE

Rotten, decaying, stripped of all senses,
they had me pinned to the floor

Left for dead, in this room I was laying,
beaten, bruised, cut and sore.

Two days had passed, there was a Doctor,
above the shit hole tavern, a room.

He fixed me up for the price of admission,
under the light of the moon.

It was a Monday in Chicago, I planned out
my vengeance, for those bastards who
left me for dead.

Just as I prepared to get my hands
dirty, A voice told me " forgive them instead.
I was totally surprised as I heard this voice
speaking,
it said " son do not be afraid "

I'm your salvation, your friend, your God till
the end, do not sleep in this bed you hath
made.

Those men whom had hurt you, left to desert you,
when alone they are kneeling to pray.

It was their mother that taught them,
for all their sin's I had bought them,

it is I whom will show them the way.

WHO IS I?

I am an enigma, a mystery machine,
I keep people guessing, what's next.

They've all sorts of questions, they bridle
the groom, I'm tricky and somewhat perplexed.

Some have the incorrect notion, feelings
are worn on my sleeve.

It's sad, they are wrong, could never belong,
with a man whom is complex like me.

Finally in closing, I would like to add,
I've a pure heart made of gold.

You'll not catch me mad, sold, sorry,
or sad, I'm a free man at sixty year's old.

THE GET OUT POEM

I feel the friction, is thick in the air,
gravity chains me to the floor

You bring the drama, the note of despair,
I bring the holes in the door

You've got me thinking, this terrible mess,
to remove you, make a new life

Your actions are stinking, your mean cold excess,
along with your baggage and strife

So" there is the door mate time to get gone,
never again will you see,

You messed up the good thing,
you burned the whole bridge, to the utmost

and dumb high degree.

SIMPLE MAN

I'm a simple man, free of frustration,
kindly I speak without doubt

All that I need, is communication,
removing the in, and the out

I trained myself in the art known as listen,
void of thinking while the other one speaks

I Steer clear of gossip, a defective condition,
the sound of it foul, and it wreaks

I've also been known to be a bit of a giver,
to a stranger, a friend, times to share

These are the traits, that make up my calling,
with meaning, I love, and I care.

PINK LIQUID

Gentle the moment, peace deep within,
take now the current, new life to begin

embracing the wonder, way down I do breath,
the wind like pink liquid, as vast as the sea

swim through the silence, the lay of the night,
roof taking rain drop's, lovely the sight

Turn now the pages, whisper the air,
fly as the wind blows, free of despair

travel a journey, remember a way,
move through the shadow's, rest through
the day

MIND GAME

You might think you know me
because you speak my name,
but you are mistaken,
my walk is a game.
I have an agenda, I'm here
for the thrill, I keep a secret
the people I kill.
I live on the border, I stay in my room
I am an outlaw, my middle name?
DOOM.
You won't see me coming, I
don't walk with grace
I won't offer mercy
as I peel off your face.
The reason I'm speaking,
the reason I'm here,
to harness my talent,
and to give all you fear.

THE ASSASSIN

I'm a deadly assassin, I kill with a skill
I'm a highly paid killer with a quota to fill

My victims are clueless, unaware of the threat,
pimp's, pusher's, and dealer's, taken off of the set.

I am wise to the street life, I know every block,
when I come calling, the door behind me gets locked.

I study the number of those in the room,
I see their weapons, I'm the bringer of doom.

After twenty four seconds, every one of them dead,
one slowly lingered, with a knife in his head.

Let this be a lesson, if it happens to you,
send ten men to greet me and I might not get through.

TO OUR LEADER'S

Hail to our leader's, lend me your ear,
we're growing tired of all that we hear.

While you are scheming, the change that you plan,
the people that suffer, the lie's in your hand.

The map to our cities, the rumors of war's,
the coup you are plotting, the fight on our shore's.

Find you some history, do what is right,
come out of the darkness, back into the light.

We the people, the Constitution we bare,
bring back the honor, what is right, what is fair.

This is a message, a warning, a timely alarm,
do away with all malice, and the people you harm.

DEVIL IN THE JUNGLE

A man encapsulated with abilities that are
inhumane, the very fabric around him is torn.

His skin is condensed into that of a hippo,
at the end of each finger a thorn.

He watched in horror as his wife and his children,
gunned down right in front of his eye's.

He had the ability to become invisible,
telepathy was no big surprise.

Wondering around, terrorized the Mekong,
his mind transcended, and free.

He became known as the devil in the jungle,
raising the dead like debris.

I HAVE NOT MONEY, WHAT I DO HAVE, GIVE I THEE

Quiet I slumber, in silence I breath, stealing one
moment, so deep like the sea.

A crack in the sidewalk, revealed there a rose,
growing in beauty, beauty it sow's.

Sweet meditation, priceless is time, all is forgotten,
the reason, the rhyme.

In you I see wonders, in you there grows peace,
take now your worries, bow to the east.

His name is holy, his word bound in truth,
he died for our sin, for me, and for you.

Fear ye the God of Adam, and Eve,
paradise is waiting, soon you shall see.

MAYBE

Bogged down with distractions, losing my flow,
the plants are all dying, no longer will grow.

Will I be accepted? will I find MY way?
or will I die? full of rot and decay.

We all have our own mountains, we all get depressed,
we all just hang in there, we all do our best.

Rarely this happens, that I get attuned, that I'm
losing desire, the weeds grow unpruned.

Maybe it's normal, maybe it's right,
to step out of the darkness, back into the light.

TITLE NOT KNOWN

As the miles turn to dust, I nary found a soul to trust.
A message found in drifting flask, begged a question
to be asked.
Little comfort can be found, envision pearls cast to
the ground.
The tempest sea which rose to kill, brought to me one final thrill.
While we sing with shouts of praise, in death a baby child lay's.
For all beginnings bring an end, two pennies for your eye's
I'll send.

STOP THE INSANITY

We are living on borrowed time.
The signs, the behavior's, the outcomes
all rest on a very weak, slippery shoulder.
The changes we all are facing, ring loudly
in our ears, forcing us to pretend that everything
is hunky dory.
The status quo, the ingredients, the pie
that is baking in the oven will be charred and
burnt.
My eyes have seen the glory of the coming
of what? of who?
When the levee breaks, our drowning cry's
will not comfort us if we
do not stop the insanity, thriving
in our world.

FORTUNE COOKIE

The path walked with wisdom will bring you
to many blessings.
The path walked with a fool, will only bring
hardships and strife.

THESE EYES

The eye's speak abruptly, giving away, the story
your begging to lose.
Some eye's look lost, drowning in sorrow,
due to the path's that we choose.
Mine tell a fable, not giving away, the apologue
deep down within.
I've come to a path narrow and thorny, training
my eye's toward my sin.
Other eye's look broken and painful, willowing
up full of tears.
Drowning in sorrow, living in hate, these eyes
have been that way for years.

THE WARRIOR'S PATH

Thoughts come in the silence, peace undisturbed,
removing the god of disdain.
Love for the weather, quiet I slumber, the sound
of the roof taking rain.
Sweet meditation, deeply I breath, enlightenment surely
will come.
In one swift motion, My hand break's the ice, to the
sound of the flute and the drum.
Breaking the silence I stand up to speak, sharing
the love I have found.
A warrior of combat, trained for the fight, my feet
planted firmly on ground.

FIND MEDITATION

Meditation, freedom, and strength from thin air.
In these things be whole and do them with care.

Now find you quiet, a place you can breathe.
Allow your frustrations and care's take their leave

Mind, body and spirit, together as one.
Find there your peace, the battle is won.

TRAINED MONKEYS

Today I was dumfounded by the speech of those
whom are fighting addiction.
It served as a reminder that some people find comfort
in their belying absurd exaggeration of stroking each other
with promises of better day's if we just hang in there.
After deliberating with what they were saying I quickly realized
how phony and weak they were, tickling each other's ears
by telling them, stay positive, don't give up!
When they were finished with these false belief's and
muddled Cliche's, I felt as though I wanted to vomit.
This encouraged me to quit keeping company of these
robot's that move and speak as if someone had flipped
a switch.
The path I have chosen calls for discipline and a deeper
understanding that I will not chant their stupid f--cking mantra's
promising a rainbow when it rains.
Hence; Trained monkeys.

SUBDUE YOUR ENEMIES

I'm standing with my enemies, they have me
surrounded.
BUT! In that circle I am preparing myself to go
to battle.
In the space between us I have room to move,
My enemy see's the weapons in my arsenal, my
short sword for up close fighting, my five ft spear
for far away targets,
My brass knuckles to deliver a beating to the
body and face.
Self-delusion takes a flurry of punches to its
ribs and throat with the brass knuckles
stopping its ability to ask for
mercy.
Self-pity is done in with cuts to its armpits
so it cannot hold its hands to its mouth, crying
poor me.
These are examples of man's true enemies,
and it's my will to capture each one and put
them in their place.

THE STUDENT SPEAKS

Life begins with a whimper, feeling the vibration of
speech. As we are fed, we grow, learning the appropriate
language to express communication to those around us.
I'm being taught from a man who's name I cannot mention.
Nor can I make any judgements, he is this, he is that ETC.
My training began with the statement " I DON'T KNOW "
So began this quest, fighting my way to enlightenment.
He has recently showed me that the warriors walk is a lonely one.
Solitude is a necessity, also the weapon of meditation, freeing
the mind, watering the sprout until it has fully grown.
There are a meticulous instructions, every stone must be
flipped over, My path is narrow, and now I am seeing there are
no people on this path with me.
Faith in what we do is an absolute must,
I am content, enlightenment will come
when it comes, things are as they are.

DIRE DEVOTION

The foundation of sand and water will cause the big house
to sink.
With shovel and plow I will clear the acre's, give what
I plant water to drink.
The gears of war are now set in motion, calling all warrior's
to fight!
To break down the walls of phony devotion, to sin's I revealed
in the light.
Now! I have something of value and worth, making my sad
life complete.
I must take cover, from the rain coming down, washing
away the ground under
my feet.

MASTER MU

This my profession, this be my will.
To break down the walls in front of me still.

Call them your mountains, or silly belief's weighing
you down till you drop.

Call them some people with poor agitation, that
rarely know how to stop.

My mind is in prison, locked up in a cell, driving me
mad too insane.

Teasing the cell with the thought to be free,
locked up is where I remain.

BUT! I have a weapon, deadly and skilled, slowly
breaking the bars that protect.

At least that's what I thought as they guarded my life,
but it was my life that they wrecked.

My weapon, a Master, trained in the art's, conceiving
a plan in the light.

Making me strong, and bringing me hope, unafraid
to get up in a fight.

He is my teacher brought to me from thin air,
a beacon that is guiding my way.

I must be careful not to insult or inside
my cell I will stay.

THE BUDDING WARRIOR'S DECREE

Right now is all there is, not yesterday, nor tomorrow.
Contentment is choice, as is joy with much sorrow.
The hands of time move forward and ticking.
I came into this world, crying, and kicking.
The negative thoughts that rise up to chain me.
Are losing this fight, which now entertain me.
I will cast them away to a place called I don't care.
No longer my master, as of now they're in nowhere.

AN AMERICAN RECIPE

Cheating while tested, gorging on crap, baby with soiled diaper
sitting high on my lap.
Complaining, with moaning, screams to be loved,
pulling my punches when push turns to shove.
Not paying my taxes, doing nothing to win, going to hell
for the weight of my sin.
This is a list of things that I'll do no more,
If I've worn out my welcome " please "
show me the door.

A Guy Walks In To An Escort Service

A woman caught up in the prostitution racket, is
severely beaten by her handler for spitting on
the face of her escort client.

The client then complains to her handler, hence,
the terrible beating.

As she lies in the serious injuries ward of the
Saint Joeseph Memorial hospital, while there
she earns a visitor whom she knows as a patron
of, Marries lounge and cafe.

While sitting in the hallway three doors down at
the coffee station a girl from the same escort service
is crying and fails miserably at filling her cup.

Now, pay attention; The visitor to see Sasha, is for
all sense and purpose an elite assassin retired from

the C I A, the girl who spilled her coffee gave him
a card which advertised the address and name of the
escort service.

Listen close, The assassin " we will call " (Mr. Smith)
decides to pay this handler for " the badly beaten Sasha "
a friendly visit.

While he knocks on this pimps disgusting door
he can hear their laughing and conduction of
business. He then enters the room, paying close
attention to their movements and to weapons
on point.

DICTIONARY

Magnanimous, a long word, found expressing courage a
forgiving style.
Walking tall when the chips roll in, packing a clean
brilliant smile.
Astute, all though short with its letters, calls for shrewdness,
and a sharp clever mind.
To see the way through a difficult path, reads completely
before the contract is signed.
Loquacious, a person endowed with an annoying gift to
speak, clueless as when it's time to stop.
Brags on his spoiled little brats, and his long winded wife,
until his legs give out to drop.
These are a few of many words I have learned, there will
be that many more.
Taking my time with the rhythm, the rhyme, that's what
a poet is for.

OLD MAN HATTEN

The streets are abandoned, the tower clock broken
no one to remember at all.

Sky scrapers are old, no words shall be spoken,
once full of life standing tall.

Down on south third street, alive with the hookers
looking to turn one more trick.

Now they're all gone, no more meth cookers,
the sight of it all makes me sick

Call it the ending, call it a plague, call it a bag full of
rocks

Call it a bitch on her thirty day rag, soaking it up
with her socks.

This marks an index, each card has been used,
a nightmare or just a bad dream?

Grab you a rag and a bottle of Windex and
clean off the shit for I scream!

MY REALITY

The fact that I am in this world " in my mind " tells me that
it must have a need for me to be in it.

Growing up I did not experience warm greetings, I did not
have the luxury of choosing where I could play.

As a young person I was taught how to hate everything around
me. I do not seek pity, I do not need to be understood, I do not

need to be liked and I do not need to be accepted.
You could probably see that I am self-absorbed counting
how many times you see the letter " I ".

There is only one thing you really need to know is that when
I was busy getting jumped at school, When I was called horrible
names, and when I was humiliated just for the way that I looked

I felt absolutely every bit of it. Now" in my adult years what I've come
to believe is I am black and white in a world full of
color.

A RIDDLE

E.A.P. begged a question, The boundaries which divide life
from death, are at best shadowy and vague.
Who shall say where one ends, and where the other
begins?
The answer is simple: " GOD "

THE CREATURE

I watched in horror as what looked to be tendrils
slithering up the wall outside my garage.

They were attached to an ugly creature that had
eye's the size of small buttons on your dress shirt.

When it opened its mouth I could see two long fang's
protruding from the back of its throat.

They seemed to be retractable with shorter teeth
behind it's lip.

It definitely was not from this world, and when
I approached it made a hissing sound which

was terrifying, then it opened its mouth and spoke;
'I traveled light years to get here, the least you

could do is offer me a martini.

FOR YOUR ENTERTAINMENT

I feel the rumble in my mind as I am now evolving.
You abandoned me and stole my soul an acquaintance I'm absolving.
As I look on stretched out sky's, I can see tomorrow.

The lie's and tricks which you deny can only bring me sorrow.
Now the trees are bearing fruit, the flowers are now growing
At night the city lights are on, like alien beams are glowing.

I will move the wall's and doors, everything wide open
Bless a stranger with what he needs, a kind word softly
spoken

MY MAD MIND

Here deep down in the constructs of mind
I search for an answer, one I can't find
I long for the ending, my race now complete.

I'm walking on fire with no shoes on my feet.
I hear there are heavens way up past one star
Quantum equation, so deep and so far.

I wait for acceptance, something I have not known.
For now I am content, for now I am grown.

YOUR PAIN IS LIKE A TWO TON STONE

Your pain is like a two ton stone, the life you
have endured..
You'd like to think you're not alone, will your soft spoken voice
be heard?
The walls you were forced to build all around you,
are so thick and ever so high.

They are a wedge between you and the father
the reasons you break down to cry.

There are no quick ways around it my friend your journey
will be long and hard.

Lean on his grace, when you pray seek his face,
he is with you wherever
you are.

I have been chastised, I walked through the fire
sifted like a bag full of wheat.

God used a minister, an imp of the devil, to
put me in a gold velvet seat.

Well we've come to the end, do not think or pretend
that he isn't watching over you.
He is patient and kind, be ye def dumb or blind
to the finish he will see you
through.

TO THE LEADERS

Life' a noun we all take for granted, some day
it will come to a stop.
With eight billion people, we share the same planet,
fighting to be on the top.

How dare you the greedy, the fake politician, lying to
gain world control.
Some day you will pay the debt that you owe us, the
debt that will swallow you
whole.

Many men, women and children in poverty, hungry
and going without.
You must have a heart that loves the people or, some day
you will thirst in the drought.

I plead will you give to the poor and the hungry how
many mouth's you could feed?
You make feel as though you are well off
I think you have more than
you need.

Awareness' a joke without any punch line, excuse
me if I fail to laugh.
There is a politician watching the counter, It's his lunch
break, he eats in the
back.

THE GOLDEN BUTTERFLY

A pretty golden butter fly, came and spit
into my eye, then she asked me was I wish

I told her no, to her surprise, She then said
you answered true, something most men

never do, She spoke a language I've not heard
I understood most every word, She pointed

to a dragon's fire, the dragon I did much admire,
I asked her then could I acquire humility

and humbleness too, she said yes before you
do, you will have to empty every thought

things like this cannot be bought, She
then said I could be taught and asked

if I was ready?

A FEATHER IN THE WIND

Consider the Komodo dragon, he will give one bite
then wait for the neuro toxins to take effect.

when the wounded animal, alive or dead has fallen
the Komodo will eat at his leisure.

This is what happens when we hurl insults at people
something I have also done.

When the insult is made, it releases things similar to
neuro toxins, I call them shame, hurt feelings, belittlement
and there are many more

Those insults cannot be taken back, A wise man once said
when we tarnish some ones character it is likened to

placing a feather on the porch on each one in the village
Then when a strong wind comes it blows them far away

Once an insult has passed, it can never be taken
back.

THE CREATURE

I watched in horror as what looked to be tendrils
slithering up the wall outside my garage.

They were attached to an ugly creature that had
eye's the size of small buttons on your dress shirt.

When it opened its mouth I could see two long fang's
protruding from the back of its throat.

They seemed to be retractable with shorter teeth
behind it's lip.

It definitely was not from this world, and when
I approached it made a hissing sound which

was terrifying, then it opened its mouth and said
'I traveled light years to get here, the least you
could do is offer me a martini.

A RIDDLE

E.A.P. begged a question, The boundaries which divide life
from death, are at best shadowy and vague.

Who shall say where one ends, and where the other
begins?

The answer is simple: " GOD "

MY REALITY

The fact that I am in this world " in my mind " tells me that
it must have a need for me to be in it.

Growing up I did not experience warm greetings, I did not
have the luxury of choosing where I could play.

As a young person I was taught how to hate everything around
me. I do not seek pity, I do need to be understood, I do

need to be liked and I do need to be accepted.
You could probably see that I am self-absorbed counting
how many times you see the letter " I ".

There is only one thing you really need to know is that when
I was busy getting jumped at school, When I was called horrible
names, and when I was humiliated just for the way that I looked

I felt absolutely every bit of it. Now" in my adult years what I've come
to believe is I am black and white in a world full of
color.

THERE IN THE LIGHT
I CAN SEE TRACES

There in the light I can see traces,
lovely smiles on kind lovely faces.

As we walk we do not tumble, hungry bellies
moan and they grumble.

Peace sublime, sins on the alter,
Like eagles we run, we nary do falter.

Find your rest there on God's mountain,
beget your healing in the cool fountain.

Forever do away with the lying,
avoid the complainers whom are not even trying

In all ye do be kind and grateful,
do not take part with those angry and hateful.

These instructions bring life, it's up to you to
apply them, you might not succeed
if you simply don't try them.

WHEN ANGELS CRY

If you could look me in the eye, you may see tears
when angel's cry.

I gave my all, I've nothing more, waves crashing
down on peaceful shores.

You are cruel, undone and bitter cold, the names
I'm called are grown and old.

The day you'd gone I was still a mess, the cuts
were deep I had to dress.

Now is the time for healing waters, as your all alone,
no sons, no daughters.

You were the worst, there'll not be another,
You were no wife, nobodies mother.

Your lost and hateful but I know why, there
are no tears when angels cry.

THE CURE

Resentments and grudges are poisonous and deadly
They are the tools of the devil, the things that
he fed me.

They make the heart hard, for evil they groom you
Like anger with hatred, they will all but consume
you.

These nabob's, these demons, influential and daunting,
When you are hooked, it's a shame and exhausting.

This is my attempt to help and to warn you, do away
with all malice and walk in some good shoes.

Pray for a change have some grace and compassion
Now you've heard the cure , put it to action.

THE TIME AT HAND

There is an enemy that wants us destroyed,
he knows he is losing and gets so annoyed.

His name is pure evil so I'll leave it blank,
And if you don't like it, you know who to thank.

He's after our souls and some are possessed,
It's a real ugly sight and you know the rest.

The time is upon us, day turn's to night,
he'll come as an angel, as a minister of light.

We're fighting our urges, we say no to sin.
He knocks on our door's but we won't let him in.

So be on your guard, we're running a race
For your protection a shield made of faith.

CREATION

What is beyond all our boundaries, how did we
all come to be
Who created the lightning and rain, who cast all
our sin's to the sea.
Who was it that gave us all creatures, who named
them all one at a time
Who was it that gave man a woman, who gave us
all love so sublime.
We all were born with the knowledge, we know
how we all came to be
Not everyone believes in the answer, not everyone
stand's to agree.

LOOK IN THE MIRROR

There is a foe, one I'm sure you have seen
This foe is unforgiving, brutal and mean.
This foe is so hungry and it needs to feed
this foe preys on hatred, and grow's like a weed.
It hungers for resentments, for guilt and for shame
This foe feeds on failure, this foe has a name.
You'll not see it coming, where it lives, where it sleeps
This foe plays a game and this foe plays for keeps.
All I have written in time will ring true
Just look in the mirror this foe might be you.

JUNGLE WILD AFRICA

What are the chances doe's a whale when she dances
find a mate in the deep.
A lion when it's hunting growling and grunting to
take down a sheep.
What would it require for a rattler a viper to swallow
its prey.
If you are bitten, no doubt you'll be shitten, a real
ugly day.
As for the cheetah runs fast and will greetcha
her canines are long
The crocks they are meaner, the worst that I've seen
there the tails are so strong.
These are just scenarios, thoughts I was thinking, so
I wrote them all down.
You be the judge here, be honest, and be clear
I won't make a sound.

GET DOWN RAP

You tried to tell me I am fake, but that's
a lie
My human spirit is eternal, it will never die.
I am not about perfection, but I strive
to be.
My blood flow's like an estuary back into
the sea.
By the undeniable belief, that I am saved,
From where I'm standing you try to judge, but
your depraved.
Now what I'm writing is a rap, my sleeves
are rolled.
The heart that beats inside of me is
solid gold.
If this dirge for those who sin, ring's true
for you.
For now this get down rap is done,
it's finally through.

SURVIVED THE SHIT

I've been beaten and bloodied, broken, abandoned
left for dead.
But I survived all the cruelty, shame, left to rot all
the bad things they said.
Now it's over the enemies rose to just to kill me and
I'm still alive.
All those losers, loud mouth, resentful, those haters
pushed me to take a dive.
Never again will I join those nabobs, that flex their
nostrils to look bad.
Now I'm rising, I'm rolling, don't need your consoling
I'm free to be glad.
No more misery, losing, bad choices or boozing,
I'm rolling clean.
Here's to good times, and sweet rhymes no one dropping
fake dimes on my scene.

THE CONDITION OF THE

HARD HEART

The heart can become hard like an old Irish stone
it then turns to be brittle like an old dug up bone.
This heart has resentments, this heart
hates the light, it's afraid to be noticed
it's a real ugly sight. This heart has no
comrades, it is always alone, this heart longs
for friendship and it waits by the phone.
This heart just needs treatment, it needs to be loved,
for someone to tell it there's hope from
above. It may take time, the road might be long,
In time it will grow healthy, it will be strong.
These are my thoughts about the shape of this
heart, sewn back together, no longer apart.

TIME STOPS

Time stops turning for those set to die
however we want them, or how hard we cry

We think on what we wanted to do and to say
Our time at the table, games we would play

We tell ourselves and others their finally at rest
We know we're not strong but we do our best

We remember the good times we had in our home
The lessons we learned, the way we have grown

For them time has stopped, where they are they don't age
They're on a new journey with no sorrow, no rage.

They have peace eternal, they never sleep,
All the good memories are the ones you
should keep

MY BIRTHDAY IS MY BEST DAY

What greater memory than the one of my birth
delivered on Valentines day.

I am so grateful and for all that it's worth
I gambled and 'boy' did it pay.

It was Valentines day while on the job I was injured
the year was 2001.

The pain in my shoulder shot straight down my back
in that moment I knew I was done.

For fourteen years my attorney was fighting, and boy! did he have driven.

While I waited I was paid, on Valentines day he got me
one million point five.

THE HEART KEEPS ON BEATING

My heart had broken many a times
the reason I write down a word and it rhymes

though it's seen cheating, lying and worst
it cannot be quenched however it thirst's

While all these things happen there's something
I've learned
the heart keeps on beating like world always turned

But I've been busy and I came to believe
It's okay to show your feelings like the ones
on your sleeve

This year I'll turn sixty on Valentines day
and I've learned to be careful with the words
that I say.

I've written three books I'm retired and more
I have been blessed with the mess on the floor

You see though it's been damaged the heart will still
live

Do not deprive the world of the love left
to give

STREETS OF DUBLIN

I drank at a pub where the men kept a razor
tucked away in their hats for a brawl

When the fighting had ended some were there
standing, while those on the floor learned to
crawl.

We made our home in the back hills of Dublin
known for the bombs where many had
died

Those whom took part their names go unspoken
while mother's hung their heads down
and cried.

This one goes out to the brave men that have fallen
their picture hangs at a church where we pray

We hope for their spirits to fly high in heaven
may we remember at least once
a day.

ALL WE DO

Allow me to divulge myself, the questions that we ask.

Living life one day at a time, is not an easy task.

Our fall from grace, the sound of thunder, mountains
we must climb.

All the day's already lived are trailing close behind.

Every memory, every action, one day we shall be judged

So the things we should have done, become our broken
crutch.

One more thing before I go in all we do be kind, if you decide
to sell your soul, the contract must be
signed

QUIET THINE HEART,

FOOD FOR THE SOUL

Silence, the quiet, peace undisturbed
watching the drops of the rain.

How to describe it there are no words choices
I cannot explain.

Our course found on rivers we take heaven by force,
angel's we may need to fight.

Bless all the givers whom feel no remorse
that live in the realms of the light.

As for the takers your welcome is worn,
doldrums no more to receive.

And on the day the curtain was torn,
salvation for all that
believe.

GUIDED BY OUR LORD

Our strength is found guided by our Lord,
we may feel him in the breeze.

Let the armies gather against our warriors
soon they'll be on their knees.

For our king came with holy promise,
so' do not fear the mass

This finest hour we unite for the fight
if we don't it shall be
our ass.

JIMMY SAVILE

How can I sum up Jimmy Savile it may be found
in the letters of his name.

Yes he was a man whom molested young ladies
it was into their mouth's that he came.

Here was a man which was known for his doggedness
famous for Jimmy will fix it.

But in the end, there's no need to pretend, he molested,
he twisted, then fucked it.

MY AMBITION

I am a poor starving poet, there is nothing unique about me.
If I have a feeling I show it there for the whole world to see.

My pieces go without saying, am I as good as the greats?
There are some due's I'm still paying, along with the poem I
create

All of my work can be measured by my sorrows, my struggles,
my strengths.

Seldom do I contrive any pleasure, not until I go through
the lengths.

This is an insight into my soul, the poet I hope to
become.

Failure has a mouth that will swallow you whole,
a splinter under the nail of your
thumb.

SMELL THE AIR OF THE CITY

City lights set off a beat
disco music vibes through the clubs

Dudes are cruising the BLVD picking up
on the rhythm of the music

not making any progress with their lame
pickup lines 'forgotten'.

THE WEIGHT OF ADDICTION

I've felt the full weight of addiction, I've lost
everything that I own.

Part of my heart 'a sorry depiction' was coursing and
hard as a stone.

My beliefs, my intentions unfounded, it wasn't
long before I lost my way.

I thought I was cool and well rounded, I was broken
and 'boy' did I pay.

If you can relate to my story, If you feel the way that
I do, my friend there is help if you want it
was there for me and it's there for
you.

You might say that you don't have a problem,
you might say that it's under control

addiction has a mouth it's a big one
when not looking will swallow
you whole.

YOU ARE LOVED

I have known countless beings drowning in pain
they fell victim to depression that drove them
to change.
Sorrow when untreated makes you tired and sick
Hard to love or to smile which is worst take
your pick.
Help is there if it's wanted it's needed we know
You will have to take the first step
with the weight you must tow.
If you're afraid my friend well I've been there
too
I will love you and embrace you for I've walked in
your shoes.
If you're not a believer you will not be judged
despite how your feeling I will love you
so much.
Well I hope this will inform you to get the help
that you need,
For a tree to start growing you must first plant
the seed.

NO PUDDING FOR PUTIN

This world although fighting with covetous igniting, preying
on woman and child.

Starting wars with those thought weaker, Putin the
tweaker walks low without
any style.

Those who say they are wiser, their dickhead advisor
will rise and the wicked will
fall.

They are damned and forsaken, they're levy is breaking
they will be dead one
and all.

They attack without warning, like a beehive their swarming
savoring the meal yet to
come.

Their souls lost forever, they thought they were clever
on the battlefield their necks
will be rung.

For the righteous are forming, and 'we'll attack without
warning' parading their heads on
a stick.

They'll be judged their transgressions, won't learn
any lessons, in the end they'll be
tired and sick

They will lose every battle, on their horse with no saddle,
kicking their shins with our
boots.

May the victorious be humble, prepare for the rumble
the Scotts play a dirge on their
flutes.

MY DAD

I was seventeen in a trade school, my sister
Debbie had called,

she spoke calmly and slowly and
then she chattered and balled.

My father was a good man, a scholar and more,
my mother found him in the bathroom lying dead
on the floor

He took his own life with a colt forty five,
I try not to picture the gun by
his side.

My father was a minister and very keen
on the word, I guess suicide is a sin at least it's
something I've heard.

There is one picture of him running up a ramp in the zoo
He was right behind me when I saw it I knew

That he was tender, loving not rough , when he played with
us children I never could get enough.

These are the memories, the thoughts that I love,
but now I know he's in heaven with Jesus
above.

This is my feeling, something I choose to believe
it's a balm, and a comfort with heavenly
peace.

I WANT GOOD THINGS FOR YOU

If your world is dark, lonely. If your station is tattered
and worn.
Come take my hand, I can see you've been battered,
deep in your side
is a thorn.
I'll never quit you, call you cruel names nor hit you,
my friend I've been where you are.
I'll give you new shoes that fit you, kill the bad dog that bit you,
play you easy songs on my
old guitar.
I've come to the finish, I'll make one sweet wish, that your
life be healthy and long.
Come out of the darkness, in the light make your own wish,
find you a place you
belong.

LIFE

A badass old school gangster, three kilos of coke
three hundred thousand reasons in a bag on
a boat.
Doing time in San Quinton on tear seventeen
doing sit ups and pushups, now I'm chiseled,
and lean.
I was driving on the backroads, on highway twenty
one,
the sunset was sinking, I had my hand on the
gun.
The destination was getting closer
I saw the lights, heard the wail, There was
no use in running
smokey was hot on my
tail.
Three strikes, with many letter's, said goodbye to
the wife
she hit the floor weeping when the judge gave
me LIFE.

MY VERSION OF HALLELUJAH

I heard the angel's sing out loud
they were there the day God tore the shroud
The day that Jesus gave his life
to save you.

The song they sung struck the devil down
and now he slivers on the ground
never again will he see the gates of
heaven.

As he hung there on the cross one man
was saved the other lost
the sins of man could finally be
forgiven.

I'll wait for you to share your love
sent to you from God above,
but for now take the peace that
God is giving.

Allow me to close with a final word
in case you forgotten or never heard
he conquered death so we could go
on living

JERRY, A PRISONER NO MORE

Jerry you're on a path bound for greatness,
let nobody stand in your way.
The obstacles, walls and frustration, in time
all the hard knocks will pay.

When you are tempted remember your journey,
how far you came to right now,
pray to your heavenly father, lean on his grace and
be proud.

Let God be your strength when you're tired,
the holy spirit will ease drops of pain.
Jesus will always be with you, a cover
when you're in the rain.

Allow me to close with a hallelujah, I praise God
for the blessings to come.
As Jesus hung on the cross dying, forgave us when
he said' it is done.

My take on not perfect

Saturday morning the weekend has arrived and I embrace
it like a friend I haven't seen in a while.
Marked with the scars and the cuts that take
a life time to mend, admonished by an adolescent
thought to be better than me, but! we all breathe
the same air.
Allow me the privilege to be a not so perfect being
that has made his fair share of mistakes, not making excuses
but if I do it's only me trying to help you to understand
that hurting you is not going to solve the greater problem
How can I fix what I've broken?
Does time really mend all wounds?
Only time can tell.

A LONG TIME

Back in the day I sat with killer's and thieves
how I survived is far beyond me.

The right hand of providence watching over
me then? saving my ass again and again.

I believe there is a power the very source of all life
you might say it's good, if you do so do I.

I won't go into details on the things that I've done
I picked up peace and put down the
gun.

TIME

Time' that elusive pretender, stops for
no man dead set on squeezing every drop
of life it can take.

Hyper drive, time speeds up not yielding
hugging the road on those tight corners
a quantum mathematical equations diverging
over itself, through time we grow, live, then
die.

For some not quite ready for departure try to cheat
time by frozen animation, maybe?
In the end time' is there, growing right alongside of you.

Time' that elusive silent partner, never dying,
never growing
old' time.

GODS CONVENIENT STORE

Your mind is so brilliant, a marvel to see
incandescent acid trip in there you are free

serenity and peace are on aisle four
right next to sorrow if you're hurting and sore

resentments and hatred I'm afraid we're all out
go to the corner if you really must pout.

Adventure and excitement, our barrel is full,
character, charmer if you want to be cool.

Power and humility, kindness and love
go ahead, try them on you'll find they'll fit like a glove.

For battle If I may suggest, a shield made from faith
A sword the spirit of his word Ephesians two verses eight

These are just a drop of all the tools in my
store
when you're running low please just' knock on
my door

Time to Kill

Here I am lying on my bed scratching my
sack of nuts
thinking about the ear candy I'm attempting to
share with anyone that would waste a couple of
minutes to read this.
mastery of nonsense,
I' mean, what else could we call it?
something to occupy and' hopefully entertain
those brave enough to gaze upon my masterpiece
leaving an indelible thought, how many points shall
we give him?
one * two * three*
Hmmmm, lots to think on
and so here we are at my brilliant ending
hoping you were at least moved a bit?
Bloody hell !
So please give a hoot and don't pollute

GOD KNOWS

Here I'm standing I'm in my own lane
this life gets crazy it drives me insane

I see the children who don't use their voice
They follow losers and make the wrong choice

I'm fifty nine now I've seen it all
I was they're fall guy so I took the fall.

This role I'm playing the responsible man
I'm shitting fire with my head in the sand.

You think you know me then let's take a walk
I've seen your lips move but I can't hear you talk.

Here I'm standing the space that I'm in
will God forgive me for the weight of my sin?

Minute to hour I'm taking it slow, my baby
steps man! just look at me go!

I'll keep the faith, I'll continue to pray,
And may God bless you on this beautiful
day.

SPEECH BEFORE THE GAME

It doesn't take much to be noble,
to blanket our thoughts in the truth.

Now we can all be forgiven, for the
God awful sins of our youth.

It's a challenge when we are discerning,
to see trouble coming. ahead

Lets do our best to avoid it,
to have a life, and not end up
dead.

*Jesus was the ultimate martyr,
he died for the weight of our sin,

He did this out of love and compassion,
Get the devil out, and let Jesus in.

AS I'M GROWING OLDER I'M
SEEING A CHANGE

As I'm growing older I'm seeing a change,
I'm wrapped up in blessings, saying goodbye to
the pain.

I've been blessed with more money, with all
that I need, my faith grows eternal, not choked out
by the weeds.

I've got food in my belly, a roof over my head,
the thought 'I'm a loser' is tired and dead.

I have three big brothers, sister in laws too,
They give me strength and they raise me,
their love sees me through.

To God, the holy spirit, to Jesus the son,
forgave our sins on the cross when he said'
'It is done'.

RECIPE FOR A GOOD LIFE

If you are struggling, bemoaning your station, change
your outlook and negative self-talk.

When you grow tired of the same old destinations,
find you a new place to walk.

Filling your mind with unwanted resentments, or jealousy
stored in your heart,

put that aside, do your best to abide, every day could be
a fresh brand new start.

Take the time the good Lord has given, do what is good,
what is right.

Get you a dose of some clean healthy livi'n,
Find you a home in the light.

As for the end of this grand crescendo, I've got one
more thing to say.

Get down on your knees, and God will be pleased,
as he hears every word that
you pray.

SMUDGE

There are two kind of people in this world
the wanna be's or the gonna be's
but there's a third, the I am's.

WAR DANCE

There are many more mountains we'll have to climb,
take my hand if you're tired, or falling behind.

We are in this together, no more standing alone,
Share our strength, ride the weather, show the master
we've grown.

Show them your war face a warrior so fierce
no time for crying you must kill your tears

The game we are playing, the rules set in place.
dig in for the battles. and lean on his grace.

These are my feelings, the thoughts that I think,
I'm sharing my knowledge on this internet ink.

I'm not claiming to have all the answers, when it's time
to show, keep your eyes on the father for the weight we must
tow.

THE SPEECH

I feel your pain and the harsh way you were treated, you felt unloved without
the kindness you needed.

So I'll move mountains, break down the walls that surround you, you were lost
but by God's grace we have found you.

This is my mission, I'll keep going till we're finished, you'll have the strength
and it won't be diminished. I'll never leave you nor will I forsake you, avoid the
things that tear you down, meant to break you.

In all you do just be happy and be grateful,
Put down the grudge and everything hateful,

Then you will have peace when all's calm quiet
What I offer is good, dig deep and buy it.

THE PROSTITUTE

Whom among us will stand in judgment,
who has the God given right
Those of you who are accusing, were seen
with her at night
Each of you cast the first stone sit high
on your fake throne, I've got some news
just for you.
Some day you shall answer, for as you spread
your cancer, you will be judged with the
truth

NO TO WINTER

Winter, cold, unforgiving, first snow,
covering the ground like a blanket.
Misery unfolds in the form of freezing
sickness, pushing, moving those whom
suffer it's embrace.
I yearn for the summers warmth, the nagging
cold, a frozen hell on earth, still the sky has revealed
sun, I jump, inwardly giving praise, let my heavenly
father smile, joy is in my
heart.

SCHEMES OF THE DEVIL

Put on the full armor of God, to shield yourselves, from the devil every day
he will attack what
is whole.
He will come as an angel of light as he seeks out to swallow your
soul.
We have a God, whom has all the right power, the kind
of power your gonna need,
come take my hand, in the darkest of hour, before he
rips out your heart just
to feed.
Someday soon, you'll feel him coming, one day soon,
he shall arrive.
When he makes himself known, you'll hear a humming,
resist him, and the fruit of
his lie.

SAD SONG

I'm lost in my memories, from a long time ago,
my dear mother taught me, we reap what we sew.

So I rebelled, though my choices, unclear,
I thought they were friends, but
they were nowhere
near.

As I grew older not much had changed, my
innocents lost, only sorrow
remained

I was not a leader, who would follow a fool?
my aesthetics, unsound, my intentions so
cruel.

I could only imagine how they would suffer
and cry,

how they would all beg for mercy, how their
pleas reached the sky.

Looking back it's all over, I mustn't dwell
within my past,

hated by my own father, and friends '

that don't last.

69 SUITS FOR SPACE

In through the outer limits, wrinkles
on my skin.
I haven't any answers for the condition
I'm in.
Vast and viewed less, acres upon acres
of psychedelic flowers,
Standing tall, I hate them all, trees stick
up like towers.
In my mind, the shit I find, all things out
of place.
The contract signed, to cruel to be kind,
the whole damn human race.
We've flown for hours, the mood here sours
the constellations wide and high,
We are breaking, the mission forsaking,
the crew's begun to cry.
So, here we are now, don't ask why now,
has the sickness start to spread?
I'm the last man standing, as the ship is landing,
in the end I'm good as dead.